The Meaning of Suffering

The Mystery of Sacrifice

Selections from the Bahá'í Holy Writings

Outlined and Compiled by Judith Hatcher

*For Bill,
a warm and loving human being*

The Meaning of Suffering

... God hath never burdened any soul beyond its power. (GL 106-107)

Outline

A. Apparent contradictions
    1. The goodness of God and the universality of grief and affliction
    2. The coexistence of joy and pain in the material world
B. Different kinds of suffering
    1. Suffering inflicted on innocent people by oppressors
    2. Suffering that we cause to others and to ourselves
    3. Suffering sent by God to the believers
    4. Sufferings of the Manifestations of God
C. The purpose of tests
    1. Preparation for the spiritual world
    2. The process of spiritual growth
    3. The method of God
    4. The principle of separation and distinction
    5. The process of purgation for humankind
D. The ways tests contribute to our spiritual growth
    1. Remember God and discover the power of prayer
    2. Detach ourselves from the material world
    3. Overcome our own egotism
    4. Learn to forgive ourselves as well as others
    5. Develop true empathy towards others
    6. Learn to sacrifice
    7. Develop patience in difficulties
    8. Accept the limits of our own understanding
    9. Learn to submit to the Divine Will
    10. Strive for true contentment
E. Promises and assurances found in the Bahá'í Writings
    1. Our point of view is extremely relative
    2. God is faithful, loving, compassionate and merciful
    3. God's mercy is greater than His justice
    4. God does not test us beyond our limits
    5. The soul is not affected by physical or mental illness
    6. Prayer is a real force, even though invisible
    7. Tests exist only in the material world
    8. The reasons for our suffering will become clear in the next life
    9. Even in this life we will experience benefits from our tests
    10. Acceptance of the Will of God leads to true happiness

A. *Apparent contradictions*

O son of man! My calamity is My providence, outwardly it is fire and vengeance, but inwardly it is light and mercy. (HW 15)

Every hair of my head proclaimeth: "But for the adversities that befall me in Thy path, how could I ever taste the divine sweetness of Thy tenderness and love?" (PM 214)

I delight in mine own afflictions and in the afflictions which they who love me suffer in Thy path. (PM 140)

Whatsoever may happen is for the best, because affliction is but the essence of bounty, and sorrow and toil are mercy unalloyed, and anguish is peace of mind, and to make a sacrifice is to receive a gift, and whatsoever may come to pass hath issued from God's grace. (SWA 257)

Wherefore, be thankful to God for having strengthened thee to aid His Cause, for having made the flowers of knowledge and understanding to spring forth in the garden of thine heart. Thus hath His grace encompassed thee, and encompassed the whole of creation. Beware, lest thou allow anything whatsoever to grieve thee. (GL 303)

… many of the perplexities that arise in your mind could be dissipated if you always conceived of the teachings as one great whole with many facets. Truth may, in covering different subjects, appear to be contradictory, and yet it is all one if you carry the thought to the end… (LG 605)

1. *The goodness of God and the universality of grief and affliction*

Do you realize how much you should thank God for His blessings? If you should thank Him a thousand times with each breath, it would not be sufficient because God has created and trained you. (DAL86 52)

…the manifold bounties of the Lord of all beings have, at all times, through the Manifestations of His divine Essence, encompasseth the earth and all that dwell therein. Not for a moment hath His grace been withheld, nor have the showers of His loving-kindness ceased to rain upon mankind. (KI 14)

… this earthly world is narrow, dark and frightful, rest cannot be imagined and happiness really is non-existent, everyone is captured in the net of sorrow, and is day and night enslaved by the chain of calamity; there is no one who is at all free or at rest from grief and affliction. (SS 75)

Such is this mortal abode: a storehouse of afflictions and suffering. It is ignorance that binds man to it, for no comfort can be secured by any soul in this world, from monarch down to the most humble commoner. If once this life should offer a man a sweet cup, a hundred bitter ones will follow; such is the condition of this world. (SWA 210)

2. The coexistence of joy and pain in the material world

In this world we are influenced by two sentiments, Joy and Pain.

Joy gives us wings! In times of joy our strength is more vital, our intellect keener, and our understanding less clouded. We seem better able to cope with the world and find our sphere of usefulness. But when sadness visits us we become weak, our strength leaves us, our comprehension is dim and our intelligence veiled. The actualities of life seem to elude our grasp, the eyes of our spirits fail to discover the sacred mysteries, and we become even as dead beings.

There is no human being untouched by these two influences; but all the sorrow and the grief that exist come from the world of matter – the spiritual world bestows only joy!

If we suffer it is the outcome of material things, and all the trials and troubles come from the world of illusion. (PT 110)

Be not grieved if thy circumstances become exacting, and problems press upon thee from all sides. Verily, thy Lord changeth grief into joy, hardship into comfort, and affliction into absolute ease. (DAL86 90)

The divine messengers come to bring joy to this earth, for this is the planet of tribulation and torment and the mission of the great masters is to turn men away from these anxieties and to infuse life with infinite joy. (SS 70)

B. Different kinds of suffering

1. Suffering inflicted on innocent people by oppressors

As to the subject of babes and children and weak ones who are afflicted by the hands of oppressors... for those souls there is a recompense in another world... that suffering is the greatest mercy of God. Verily, that mercy of the Lord is far better than all the comfort of this world and the growth and development appertaining to this place of mortality. (DAL86 89)

These events happen in order that man's faith may be increased and strengthened. Therefore, although we feel sad and disheartened, we must supplicate God to turn our hearts to the kingdom and pray for these departed souls with faith in His infinite mercy so that, although they have been deprived of this earthly life, they may enjoy a new existence in the supreme mansions of the Heavenly Father. (DAL86 6)

2. Suffering that we cause to others and to ourselves

If a man eats too much, he ruins his digestion; if he takes poison he becomes ill or dies. If a person gambles he will lose his money; if he drinks too much he will lose his equilibrium. All these sufferings are caused by the man himself, it is quite clear therefore that certain sorrows are the result of our own deeds. (PT 41)

3. Suffering sent by God to the believers

... sufferings there are, which come upon the Faithful of God. Consider the great sorrows endured by Christ and His apostles!

Those who suffer most, attain to the greatest perfection.

Those who declare a wish to suffer much for Christ's sake must prove their sincerity; those who proclaim their longing to make great sacrifices can only prove their truth by their deeds. Job proved the fidelity of his love for God by being faithful through his great adversity, as well as during the prosperity of his life. (PT 42)

Be content with that which God hath ordained for thee. He, verily, payeth the due recompense of those who are patient. Hast thou not seen My incarceration, My affliction, My injury, My suffering? Follow then the ways of Thy Lord, and among His methods is the suffering of His well-favoured servants. (FG 169)

4. Sufferings of the Manifestations of God

Suffering, of one kind or another, seems to be the portion of man in this world. Even the Beloved ones, the Prophets of God, have never been exempt from the ills that are to be found in our world... (LG 604-605)

How could they (God's teachers) teach and guide others in the way if they themselves did not undergo every species of suffering to which other human beings are subjected? (SS 19)

You must always remember that the Manifestations of God, Themselves, were not immune to suffering of the most human nature; and that from the hands of their relatives, they drank the bitterest potions, Bahá'u'lláh even being proffered poison by His half-brother, Mírzá Yahyá. Besides their afflictions, our afflictions, however terrible for us, must seem small in comparison. (FG 187-188)

Every morning I arose from My bed, I discovered the hosts of countless afflictions massed behind My door; and every night when I lay down, lo! My heart was torn with agony at what it had suffered from the fiendish cruelty of its foes. With every piece of bread the Ancient Beauty breaketh is coupled the assault of a fresh affliction, and with every drop He drinketh is mixed the bitterness of the most woeful of trials. He is preceded in every step He taketh by an army of unforeseen calamities, while in His rear follow legions of agonizing sorrows. (GL 119-120)

Praised be Thou, O Lord my God! Thou seest my poverty and my misery, my troubles and my needs, my utter helplessness and my extreme lowliness, my lamentations and my bitter wailing, the anguish of my soul and the afflictions which beset me. (PM 139)

12

C. The purpose of tests

1. Preparation for the spiritual world

The Prophets and the Messengers of God have been sent down for the sole purpose of guiding mankind to the straight Path of Truth. The purpose underlying Their revelation hath been to educate all men, that they may, at the hour of death, ascend, in the utmost purity and sanctity and with absolute detachment, to the throne of the Most High. (GL 156–157)

Man's physical existence on this earth is a period during which the moral exercise of his free will is tried and tested in order to prepare his soul for the other worlds of God, and we must welcome affliction and tribulations as opportunities for improvement in our eternal selves. (LG 368)

Know then that the Lord God possesseth invisible realms which the human intellect can never hope to fathom nor the mind of man conceive. When once thou hast cleansed the channel of thy spiritual sense from the pollution of this worldly life, then wilt thou breathe in the sweet scents of holiness that blow from the blissful bowers of that heavenly land. (SWA 195)

2. The process of spiritual growth

Tests are benefits from God, for which we should thank Him. Grief and sorrow do not come to us by chance, they are sent to us by the Divine Mercy for our own perfecting. (PT 42)

The mind and spirit of man advance when he is tried by suffering.... suffering and tribulation free man from the petty affairs of this worldly life until he arrives at a state of complete detachment. His attitude in this world will be that of divine happiness. Man is, so to speak, unripe: the heat of the fire of suffering will mature him. (DAL86 86)

Unless one accept suffering, undergo trials and endure vicissitudes, he will reap no reward nor will he attain success and prosperity. Therefore, thou must likewise endure great tests so that the infinite divine outpourings may encircle thee and that thou mayest be assisted in spreading the fragrances of God. (SS 22-23)

I am not impatient of calamity in His way nor of affliction for His love. God hath made afflictions as a morning shower to His green pasture, and as a wick for His lamp, whereby earth and Heaven are illumined. (JC 56)

3. The method of God

Know ye that trials and tribulations have, from time immemorial, been the lot of the chosen Ones of God and His beloved, and such of His servants as are detached from all else but Him, they whom neither merchandise nor traffic beguile from the remembrance of the Almighty, they that speak not till He hath spoken, and act according to His commandment. Such is God's method carried into effect of old, and such will it remain in the future. Blessed are the steadfastly enduring, they that are patient under ills and hardships, who lament not over anything that befalleth them, and who tread the path of resignation. (GL 129)

... from time immemorial even unto eternity the Almighty hath tried, and will continue to try, His servants, so that light may be distinguished from darkness, truth from falsehood, right from wrong, guidance from error, happiness from misery, and roses from thorns. (KI 8)

4. The principle of separation and distinction

He hath endowed every soul with the capacity to recognize the signs of God. (GL 105-106)

He Who is the Day Spring of Truth is, no doubt, fully capable of rescuing from such remoteness wayward souls and of causing them to draw nigh unto His court and attain His presence.... His purpose, however, is to enable the pure in spirit and the detached in heart to ascend, by virtue of their own innate powers, unto the shores of the Most Great Ocean, that thereby they who seek the Beauty of the All-Glorious may be distinguished and separated from the wayward and perverse.... [this] should be attributed to this same principle of separation and distinction which animateth the Divine Purpose. (GL 71)

As to tests, these are inevitable.... Is it, then, possible to be saved from the trials of God? Nay, by the righteousness of the Lord! There is a great wisdom therein of which no one is aware save the wise and knowing.

Were it not for tests, pure gold could not be distinguished from the impure. Were it not for tests, the courageous could not be separated from the cowardly. Were it not for tests, the people of faithfulness could not be known from the disloyal. (DAL86 86-87)

But for the tribulations which are sustained in Thy path, how could Thy true lovers be recognized; and were it not for the trials which are born for love of Thee, how could the station of such as yearn for Thee be revealed?... The companions of all who adore Thee are the tears they shed, and the comforters of such as seek Thee are the groans they utter, and the food of them who haste to meet Thee is the fragments of their broken hearts. (PM 155)

5. The process of purgation for humankind

You seem to complain about the calamities, that have befallen humanity. In the spiritual development of man a stage of purgation is indispensable, for it is while passing through it that the over-rated material needs are made to appear in their proper light. Unless society learns to attribute more importance to spiritual matters, it would never be fit to enter the golden era foretold by Bahá'u'lláh. The present calamities are parts of this process of purgation, [and] through them alone will man learn his lesson. They are to teach the nations, that they have to view things internationally, they are to make the individual attribute more importance to his moral, than his material welfare.

In such a process of purgation, when all humanity is in the throes of dire suffering, the Bahá'ís should not hope to remain unaffected. (LG 134)

Adversity, prolonged, world-wide, afflictive, allied to chaos and universal destruction, must needs convulse the nations, stir the conscience of the world, disillusion the masses, precipitate a radical change in the very conception of society, and coalesce ultimately the disjointed, the bleeding limbs of mankind into one body, single, organically united, and indivisible. (PDC 122-123)

D. The ways tests contribute to our spiritual growth

1. Remember God and discover the power of prayer

While a man is happy, he may forget his God; but when grief comes and sorrows overwhelm him, then will be remember his Father Who is in Heaven, and Who is able to deliver him from his humiliations. (DAL86 86)

He indeed is acceptable, O my God, who hath set his face towards Thee, and he is truly deprived who hath been careless of the remembrance of Thee in Thy days. Blessed is he that hath tasted of the sweetness of Thy remembrance and praise. (PM 205)

Were I to inherit from Thee the delights of Paradise, and to keep them in my possession as long as Thine own Being endureth, and were I to become, for less than a moment careless of the remembrance of Thee, I would, of a certainty, cast them away from me and cease to consider them. (PM 205)

The healer of all thine ills is remembrance of Me, forget it not. Make My love thy treasure and cherish it even as thy very sight and life. (HW 33)

2. Detach ourselves from the material world

Were the world to last as long as Thine own kingdom will last, to set their affections upon it would still be unseemly for such as have quaffed, from the hands of Thy mercy, the wine of Thy presence; how much more when they recognize its fleetingness and are persuaded of its transience. The chances that overtake it, and the changes to which all things pertaining unto it are continually subjected, attest its impermanence. (PM 116)

Whenever you see tremendous personal problems in your private lives…you must remember that these afflictions are part of human life; and, according to our teachings one of their wisdoms is to teach us the impermanence of this world and the permanence of the spiritual bonds that we establish with God, His Prophet, and those who are alive in the faith of God. (FG 187)

Thou wilt never cause tribulations to befall any soul unless Thou desirest to exalt his station in Thy celestial Paradise and to buttress his heart in this earthly life with the bulwark of Thine all-compelling power, that it may not become inclined towards the vanities of this world. Indeed Thou are well aware that under all conditions I would cherish the remembrance of Thee far more than the ownership of all that is in the heavens and on the earth. (BP 226)

3. *Overcome our own egotism*

This test… removes the rust of egotism from the mirror of the heart until the Sun of Truth may shine therein. For no veil is greater than egotism and no matter how thin that covering may be, yet it will finally veil man entirely and prevent him from receiving a portion from the eternal bounty. (DAL74 90-91)

When one is released from the prison of self, that is, indeed, freedom! For self is the greatest prison.

When this release takes place one can never be imprisoned. Unless one accepts dire vicissitudes, not with dull resignation, but with radiant acquiescence, one cannot attain this freedom. (DAL86 65)

Tests are a means by which a soul is measured as to its fitness, and proven out by its own acts. God knows its fitness beforehand, and also its unpreparedness, but man, with an ego, would not believe himself unfit unless proof were given to him. Consequently his susceptibility to evil is proven to him when he falls into the tests, and the tests are continued until the soul realizes its own unfitness, then remorse and regret tend to root out the weakness.

The same test comes again in greater degree, until it is shown that a former weakness has become a strength, and the power to overcome evil has been established. (SS 14)

4. *Learn to forgive ourselves as well as others*

Let us not keep on forever with our fancies and illusions, with our analyzing and interpreting and circulating of complex dubieties. Let us put aside all thoughts of self; let us close our eyes to all on earth, let us neither make known our sufferings nor complain of our wrongs. Rather let us become oblivious of our own selves, and drinking down the wine of heavenly grace, let us cry out our joy, and lose ourselves in the beauty of the All-Glorious. (SWA 247)

O Brethren! Be forbearing one with another and set not your affections on things below. Pride not yourselves in your glory, and be not ashamed of abasement. (HW 39)

O Son of Man! Breathe not the sins of others as long as thou art thyself a sinner. (HW 10)

5. Develop true empathy towards others

Often physical sickness draws man nearer unto his Maker, suffers his heart to be made empty of all worldly desires until it becomes tender and sympathetic toward all sufferers and compassionate to all creatures. Although physical diseases cause man to suffer temporarily, yet they do not touch his spirit. Nay, rather they contribute toward the divine purpose; that is, spiritual susceptibilities will be created in his heart. (JC 110)

It is incumbent upon thee, since thou hast attained the knowledge of God and His love, to sacrifice thy spirit and all thy conditions for the life of the world, bearing every difficulty for the comfort of the souls, sinking to the depth of the sea of ordeals for the sake of the love of faithfulness. (DAL74 73)

Concern yourselves with one another. Help along one another's projects and plans. Grieve over one another. Let none in the whole country go in need. Befriend one another until ye become as a single body, one and all... (SS 84)

6. Learn to sacrifice

Self-sacrifice means to subordinate this lower nature and its desires to the more Godly and noble side of our selves. Ultimately, in its highest sense, self-sacrifice means to give our will and our all to do with as He pleases. Then He purifies and glorifies our true self until it becomes a shining and wonderful reality. (SS 44)

Until a being setteth his foot in the plane of sacrifice, he is bereft of every favor and grace; and this plane of sacrifice is the realm of dying to the self, that the radiance of the living God may then shine forth. (DAL86 68-69)

The mystery of "ransom" or sacrifice is a most great subject and is inexhaustible. (DAL86 67)

7. Develop patience in difficulties

O army of God! When calamity striketh, be ye patient and composed. However afflictive your sufferings may be, stay ye undisturbed, and with perfect confidence in the abounding grace of God, brave ye the tempest of tribulations and fiery ordeals. (SWA 79)

As these tribulations, however, were sustained in Thy path and for love of Thee, they who were afflicted by them render thanks, under all conditions, unto Thee, and say: "O Thou who art the Delight of our hearts and the Object of our adoration! Were the clouds of Thy decree to rain down upon us the darts of affliction, we would, in our love for Thee, refuse to be impatient. We would yield Thee praise and thanksgiving, for we have recognized and are persuaded that Thou hast ordained only that which will be best for us. If our bodies be, at times, weighed down by our troubles, yet our souls rejoice with exceeding gladness." (PM 135)

We must not only be patient with others, infinitely patient!, but also with our own poor selves, remembering that even the Prophets of God sometimes got tired and cried out in despair! (UD 456)

8. Accept the limits of our own understanding

The prayers which were revealed to ask for healing apply both to physical and spiritual healing. Recite them, then, to heal both the soul and the body. If healing is right for the patient, it will certainly be granted; but for some ailing persons, healing would only be the cause of other ills, and therefore wisdom doth not permit an affirmative answer to the prayer. (SWA 170)

In every suffering one can find a meaning and a wisdom. But it is not always easy to find the secret of that wisdom. It is sometimes only when all our suffering has passed that we become aware of its usefulness. What man considers to be evil turns often to be a cause of infinite blessings. And this is due to his desire to know more than he can. God's wisdom is, indeed, inscrutable to us all, and it is no use pushing too far trying to discover that which shall always remain a mystery to our mind. (UD 434)

9. Learn to submit to the Divine Will

Blessed is the man that hath acknowledged his belief in God and in His signs, and recognized that "He shall not be asked of His doings." Such a recognition hath been made by God the ornament of every belief, and its very foundation. Upon it must depend the acceptance of every goodly deed....

Whoso hath not recognized this sublime and fundamental verity, and hath failed to attain this most exalted station, the winds of doubt will agitate him... He that hath acknowledged this principle will be endowed with the most perfect constancy.... Such is the teaching which God bestoweth on you, a teaching that will deliver you from all manner of doubt and perplexity.
(GL 86-87)

... Thou hast ordained that the utmost limit to which they who lift their hearts to Thee can rise is the confession of their powerlessness to enter the realms of Thy holy and transcendent unity, and that the highest station which they who aspire to know Thee can reach is the acknowledgment of their impotence to attain the retreats of Thy sublime knowledge... (PM 89)

10. Strive for true contentment

Lament not in your hours of trial, neither rejoice therein; seek ye the Middle Way which is the remembrance of Me in your afflictions and reflection over that which may befall you in future. (KA 35)

Supply them, then, from Thy sea of certainty with what will calm the agitation of their hearts. (PM 283)

I beg of Thee, O my God...to ordain that my choice be conformed to Thy choice and my wish to Thy wish, that I may be entirely content with that which Thou didst desire, and be wholly satisfied with what Thou didst destine for me by Thy bounteousness and favor. (PM 54)

You must not injure yourselves or commit suicide.... Should anyone at anytime encounter hard or perplexing times, he must say to himself, "This will soon pass." Then he will be calm and quiet. In all my calamity and difficulties I used to say to myself, "This will pass away." Then I became patient. (SS 21)

E. Promises and assurances found in the Bahá'í Writings

1. Our point of view is extremely relative

Never lose thy trust in God. Be thou ever hopeful, for the bounties of God never cease to flow upon man. If viewed from one perspective they seem to decrease, but from another they are full and complete. Man is under all conditions immersed in a sea of God's blessings. Therefore, be not hopeless under any circumstances, but rather be firm in thy hope. (SWA 215)

2. God is faithful, loving, compassionate and merciful

Verily, the will of God engages occasionally in some matter for which mankind is unable to find out the reason. The causes and reasons shall appear. Trust in God and confide in Him, and resign thyself to the will of God. Verily, thy God is affectionate, compassionate and merciful. He will look at thee with the glances of the eye of mercifulness, will guard thee with the eye of bounty, and will cause His mercy to descend upon thee. (DAL74 59)

3. God's mercy is greater than His justice

The tenderness of Thy mercy, O my Lord, surpasseth the fury of Thy wrath, and Thy loving-kindness exceedeth Thy hot displeasure, and Thy grace excelleth Thy justice. (PM 136)

Wert Thou to regard Thy servants according to their deserts in Thy days, they would assuredly merit naught except Thy chastisement and torment. Thou art, however, the One Who is of great bounteousness, Whose grace is immense. Look not down upon them, O my God, with the glance of Thy justice, but rather with the eyes of Thy tender compassions and mercies. Do, then, with them according to what beseemeth Thy generosity and bountiful favor. (PM 137)

4. God does not test us beyond our limits

He will never deal unjustly with anyone, neither will He task a soul beyond its power. He, verily, is the Compassionate, the All-Merciful. (GL 106)

… God hath never burdened any soul beyond its power. (GL 106-107)

Nothing save that which profiteth them can befall My loved ones. (SS 20)

Thou lookest upon them that are dear to Thee with the eyes of Thy loving kindness, and sendest down for them only that which will profit them through Thy grace and Thy gifts. (PM 239)

5. The soul is not affected by physical or mental illness

Know thou that the soul of man is exalted above, and is independent of all infirmities of body or mind. That a sick person showeth signs of weakness is due to the hindrances that interpose themselves between his soul and his body, for the soul itself remaineth unaffected by any bodily ailments…. every malady afflicting the body of man is an impediment that preventeth the soul from manifesting its inherent might and power. When it leaveth the body, however, it will evince such ascendancy, and reveal such influence as no force on earth can equal. (GL 153-154)

6. Prayer is a real force, even though invisible

Let us turn our hearts away from the world of matter and live in the spiritual world! It alone can give us freedom! If we are hemmed in by difficulties we have only to call on God, and by His great Mercy we shall be helped. (PT 111)

God will answer the prayer of every servant if that prayer is urgent. His mercy is vast, illimitable. He answers the prayers of all His servants….

But we ask for things which the divine wisdom does not desire for us, and there is no answer to our prayer. His wisdom does not sanction what we wish…. But whatever we ask for,

which is in accord with divine wisdom, God will answer.
Assuredly! (DAL86 51)

… not everyone achieves easily and rapidly the victory over
self. What every believer, new or old, should realise is that the
Cause *has* the spiritual power to recreate us if we make the
effort to let that power influence us, and the greatest help in
this respect is prayer. (UD 442)

Supplication and prayer on behalf of others will surely be
effective. (SW vol VIII, no 4, 47)

7. Tests exist only in the material world

…the tests and trials of God take place in this world, not in the
world of the Kingdom. (SWA 204)

…all the sorrow and the grief that exist come from the world of
matter — the spiritual world bestows only the joy!
    If we suffer it is the outcome of material things, and all
the trials and troubles come from this world of illusion…. The
trials which beset our every step, all our sorrow, pain, shame
and grief are born in the world of matter; whereas the spiritual
Kingdom never causes sadness. (PT 110)

Do not grieve at the afflictions and calamities that have befallen
thee. All calamities and afflictions have been created for man
so that he may spurn this mortal world — a world to which
he is much attached. When he experienceth severe trials and
hardships, then his nature will recoil and he will desire the
eternal realm — a realm which is sanctified from all afflictions
and calamities. (SWA 250)

8. The reasons for our suffering will become clear in the next life

When the human soul soareth out of this transient heap of dust
and riseth into the world of God, then veils will fall away, and
verities will come to light, and all things unknown before will
be made clear, and hidden truths be understood. (SWA 186)

Be not in despair, but rather smile by the mercy of thy Lord; and
be not sorrowful when meeting with worldly difficulties and

depressions, for they pass away — and thine shall be immortality during ages and centuries, times and cycles. (SS 23)

...once he hath departed this life, he will behold in that world, whatsoever was hidden from him here: but there he will look upon and comprehend all things with his inner eye.
(SWA 179-180)

9. Even in this life we will experience benefits from our tests

O My servants! Sorrow not if, in these days and on this earthly plane, things contrary to your wishes have been ordained and manifested by God, for days of blissful joy, of heavenly delight, are assuredly in store for you. Worlds, holy and spiritually glorious, will be unveiled to your eyes. You are destined by Him, in this world and hereafter, to partake of their benefits, to share in their joys, and to obtain a portion of their sustaining grace. (GL 329)

If thy daily living become difficult, soon (God) thy Lord will bestow upon thee that which will satisfy thee. Be patient in the time of affliction and trial, endure every difficulty and hardship with a dilated heart, attracted spirit and eloquent tongue in remembrance of the Merciful. Verily this is the life of satisfaction, the spiritual existence, heavenly repose, divine benediction and the celestial table! Soon thy Lord will extenuate thy straitened circumstances even in this world.
(DAL74 93)

10. Acceptance of the Will of God leads to true happiness

Afflictions and troubles are due to the state of not being content with what God has ordained for you. If one submits himself to God he is happy.... When man surrenders himself everything will move according to his wish. (DAL76 10)

Contentment is real wealth. If one develops within himself the quality of contentment he will become independent. Contentment is the creator of happiness. When one is contented he does not care either for riches or poverty. He lives above the influence of them and is indifferent to them. (attributed to 'Abdu'l-Bahá; FG 171)

Man must so live that he may become beloved in the sight of God, beloved in the estimation of the righteous ones and beloved and praised by the people. When he reaches this station the feast of eternal happiness is spread before him. His heart is serene and composed because he finds himself accepted at the threshold of His Highness, the One. His soul is in the utmost felicity and bliss even if he be surrounded by mountains of tests and difficulties. He will be like a sea on the surface of which one may see huge white waves, but in its deeps it is calm, unruffled and undisturbed. (SS 60)

The Mystery of Sacrifice

The mystery of "ransom" or sacrifice is a most great subject and is inexhaustible. (DAL86 67)

…to make a sacrifice is to receive a gift (SWA 257)

Outline

A. Suffering and sacrifice
1. The universality of suffering
2. God's method with respect to the believers
3. The principle that will "endow constancy"
4. Learning to sacrifice: one of the purposes of suffering

B. The mystery of sacrifice
1. The meanings of sacrifice
2. Self-sacrifice
3. Sacrifice and faithfulness
4. Ransom and sacrifice
5. The law of sacrifice

C. The Manifestations of God and the law of sacrifice
1. The Manifestation of God
2. Jesus Christ
3. Abraham and Muhammad
4. The Báb
5. Bahá'u'lláh

D. The believers and the law of sacrifice
1. 'Abdu'l-Bahá, the perfect exemplar
2. The believers

E. The consequences of sacrifice
1. Transforms personal effort into spiritual qualities
2. Has a positive spiritual influence on others
3. Helps give meaning to tests and difficulties
4. Releases spiritual power into the world

A. Suffering and sacrifice

1. The universality of suffering

Suffering, of one kind or another, seems to be the portion of man in this world. Even the Beloved ones, the Prophets of God, have never been exempt from the ills that are to be found in our world; poverty, disease, bereavement—they seem to be part of the polish God employs to make us finer, and enable us to reflect more of His attributes! No doubt in the future, when the foundation of society is laid according to the Divine plan, and men become truly spiritualized, a vast amount of our present ills and problems will be remedied. We who toil now are paving the way for a far better world, and this knowledge must uphold and strengthen us through every trial. (LG 604-605)

2. God's method with respect to the believers

Know ye that trials and tribulations have, from time immemorial, been the lot of the chosen Ones of God and His beloved, and such of His servants as are detached from all else but Him, they whom neither merchandise nor traffic beguile from the remembrance of the Almighty, they that speak not till He hath spoken, and act according to His commandments. Such is God's method carried into effect of old, and such will it remain in the future. Blessed are the steadfastly enduring, they that are patient under ills and hardships, and who lament not over anything that befalleth them, and who tread the path of resignation. (GL 129)

We hear thy cry and supplication at thy remoteness from the Dawning-Place of Lights. Be patient and do not bewail thy plight. Be content with that which God hath ordained for thee. He, verily, payeth the due recompense of those who are patient. Hast thou not seen My incarceration, My affliction, My injury, My suffering? Follow then the ways of thy Lord, and among His methods is the suffering of His well-favored servants. (FG 169)

3. The principle that will "endow constancy"

Blessed is the man that hath acknowledged his belief in God
and in His signs, and recognized that "He shall not be asked
of His doings." Such a recognition hath been made by God the
ornament of every belief, and its very foundation. Upon it must
depend the acceptance of every goodly deed....

He that hath acknowledged this principle will be endowed
with the most perfect constancy. Such is the teaching which
God bestoweth upon you, a teaching which will deliver you
from all manner of doubt and perplexity, and enable you to
attain unto salvation in both this world and in the next. (GL
86-87)

4. Learning to sacrifice: one of the purposes of suffering

Other sufferings there are, which come upon the Faithful of
God. Consider the great sorrows endured by Christ and by His
apostles!

Those who suffer most, attain to the greatest perfection.

Those who declare a wish to suffer much for Christ's sake
must prove their sincerity; those who proclaim their longing to
make great sacrifices can only prove their truth by their deeds.
(PT 42)

Nor shall the seeker reach his goal unless he sacrifice all things.
That is, whatever he hath seen, and heard, and understood, all
must he set at naught, that he may enter the realm of the spirit,
which is the City of God. Labor is needed, if we are to seek
Him; ardor is needed, if we are to drink of the honey of reunion
with Him; and if we taste of this cup, we shall cast away the
world. (SV 7)

B. The mystery of sacrifice

1. The meanings of sacrifice

The mystery of "ransom" or sacrifice is a most great subject and is inexhaustible.

Briefly it is as follows: The moth is a sacrifice to the candle. The spring is a sacrifice to the thirsty one. The sincere lover is a sacrifice to the loved one, and the longing one is a sacrifice to the beloved. The point lies in this: He must wholly forget himself.... He must seek the good pleasure of the True One, desire the face of the True One, and walk in the path of the True One.... This is the first station of sacrifice.

The second station of sacrifice is as follows: Man must become... like unto the iron thrown within the furnace of fire. The qualities of iron, such as blackness, coldness and solidity, which belong to the earth, disappear and vanish, while the characteristics of fire, such as redness, glowing and heat, which belong to the kingdom, become apparent and visible. Therefore, iron hath sacrificed its qualities and grades to the fire, acquiring the virtues of that element. (DAL86 67-68)

... Christ, who is the Word of God, sacrificed Himself. This has two meanings, an apparent and an esoteric meaning. The outward meaning is this:... He arose to teach and educate men, and so He sacrificed Himself to give the spirit of life. He perished in body so as to quicken others by the spirit.

The second meaning of sacrifice is this: Christ was like a seed, and this seed sacrificed its own form so that the tree might grow and develop. Although the form of the seed was destroyed, its reality became apparent in perfect majesty and beauty in the form of a tree. (SAQ 120-121)

... man must sacrifice the qualities and attributes of the world of nature for the qualities and attributes of the world of God. (DAL86 68)

The mystery of sacrifice is that man should sacrifice all his conditions for the divine station of God. The station of God is mercy, kindness, forgiveness, sacrifice, favour, grace and giving

life to the spirits and lighting the fire of His love in the hearts
and arteries. (LG 117-118)

2. Self-sacrifice

...self has really two meanings, or is used in two senses, in
the Bahá'í writings; one is self, the identity of the individual
created by God. This is the self mentioned in such passages as
"he hath known God who hath known himself etc." The other
self is the ego, the dark, animalistic heritage each one of us has,
the lower nature that can develop into a monster of selfishness,
brutality, lust, and so on. It is this self we must struggle against,
or this side of our natures, in order to strengthen and free the
spirit within us and help it to attain perfection.

Self-sacrifice means to subordinate this lower nature and
its desires to the more godly and noble side of ourselves.
Ultimately, in its highest sense, self-sacrifice means to give
our will and our all to God to do with as He pleases. Then he
purifies and glorifies our true self until it becomes a shining
and wonderful reality. (LG 113-14)

Until a being setteth his foot in the plane of sacrifice, he is
bereft of every favor and grace; and this plane of sacrifice is the
realm of dying to the self, that the radiance of the living God
may then shine forth.... Do all ye can to become wholly weary
of self, and bind yourselves to that Countenance of Splendors;
and once you have reached such heights of certitude, ye will
find, gathered within your shadow, all created things. This
is boundless grace; this is the highest sovereignty; this is the
life that dieth not. All else save this is at the last but manifest
perdition and great loss. (SWA 76-77)

With reference to what is meant by an individual becoming
entirely forgetful of self: the intent is that he should rise up and
sacrifice himself in the true sense, that is, he should obliterate
the promptings of the human condition, and rid himself of
such characteristics as are worthy of blame and constitute
the gloomy darkness of this life on earth — not that he should
allow his physical health to deteriorate and his body to become
infirm. (SWA 189)

3. Sacrifice and faithfulness

One of the requirements of faithfulness is that thou mayest sacrifice thyself and, in the divine path, close thine eye to every pleasure and strive with all thy soul that that thou mayest disappear and be lost, like unto a drop, in the ocean of God's love. (DAL74 74)

It is incumbent upon thee, since thou hast attained the knowledge of God and His love, to sacrifice thy spirit and all thy conditions for the life of the world, bearing every difficulty for the comfort of the world, sinking to the depth of the sea of ordeals for the sake of faithfulness.... (DAL74 73)

The condition of Faith requires that man ascend to and abide in the station of sacrifice. Without this attainment, one's faith is not perfect. The believers must soar toward the summit of self-sacrifice. (SW VOL V, NO 8, 118)

You were sure that if one tried to hurt her [the Greatest Holy Leaf] she would wish to console him for his own cruelty. For her love was unconditioned, could penetrate disguise and see hunger behind the mask of fury, and she knew that the most brutal self is secretly hoping to find gentleness in another....

Something greater than forgiveness she had shown in meeting the cruelties and strictures in her own life. To be hurt and to forgive is saintly but far beyond this is the power to comprehend and not be hurt.... She was never known to complain or lament. It was not that she made the best of things, but that she found in everything, even in calamity itself, the germs of enduring wisdom. She did not resist the shocks and upheavals of life and she did not run counter to obstacles. She was never impatient. She was as incapable of impatience as she was of revolt. But this was not so much long-sufferance as it was quiet awareness of the forces that operate in the hours of waiting and inactivity.

Always she moved with the larger rhythm, the wider sweep, toward the ultimate goal. Surely, confidently, she followed the circle of her orbit around the Sun of her existence, in that complete acquiescence, that perfect accord, which underlies faith itself. (BW 182-85)

37

4. Ransom and sacrifice

No man can ever claim to have comprehended the nature of the hidden and manifold grace of God; none can fathom His all-embracing mercy. Such hath been the perversity of men and their transgressions, so grievous have been the trials that have afflicted the Prophets of God and their chosen ones, that all mankind deserveth to be tormented and to perish. God's hidden and most loving providence, however, hath, through both visible and invisible agencies, protected and will continue to protect it from the penalty of its wickedness. (GL 76)

Fix your gaze upon Him Who is the Temple of God amongst men. He, in truth, hath offered up His life as a ransom for the redemption of the world. (GL 315)

May my spirit be a sacrifice to the wrongs Thou didst suffer, and my soul be a ransom for the adversities Thou didst sustain. (BP 331)

Likewise, when the souls are released from the fetters of the world, the imperfections of mankind and the animalistic darkness and have... partaken a share from the outpouring of the placeless and have acquired Lordly perfections, they are the "ransomed ones" of the Sun of Truth. (DAL74 73)

5. The law of sacrifice

With reference to your question as to whether individuals can help each other by accepting to suffer for each other's sake, surely such sacrifices for our fellow-humans can have helpful results. The law of sacrifice operates in our own lives, as well as in the lives of the Divine Manifestations. (LG 118)

C. The Manifestations of God and the law of sacrifice

1. The Manifestation of God

As to those souls who are born into this life as ethereal and radiant entities and yet, on account of their handicaps and trials, are deprived of great and real advantages, and leave the world without having lived to the full – certainly this is a cause for grieving. This is the reason why the universal Manifestations of God unveil Their countenances to man, and endure every calamity and sore affliction, and lay down their lives as a ransom; it is to make these very people, the ready ones, the ones who have capacity, to become dawning points of light, and to bestow upon them the life that fadeth never. This is the true sacrifice: the offering of oneself, even as did Christ, as a ransom for the life of the world. (SWA 69)

2. Jesus Christ

Know thou that when the Son of Man yielded up His breath to God, the whole creation wept with a great weeping. By sacrificing Himself, however, a fresh capacity was infused into all created things.... The deepest wisdom which the sages have uttered, the profoundest learning which any mind hath unfolded, the arts which the ablest hands have produced, the influence exerted by the most potent of rulers, are but manifestations of the quickening power released by His transcendent, His all-pervasive, and resplendent Spirit. (GL 85-86)

3. Abraham and Muhammad

The Voice of God commandeth Him (Abraham) to offer up Ishmael as a sacrifice, so that His steadfastness in the Faith of God and his detachment from all else but Him may be demonstrated unto men. The purpose of God, moreover, was to sacrifice him as a ransom for the sins and iniquities of all the peoples of the earth. This same honor, Jesus, the Son of Mary, besought the one true God, exalted be His name and glory, to confer upon Him. For the same reason was Husayn offered up as a sacrifice by Muhammad, the Apostle of God. (GL 75-76)

4. The Báb

Methinks He, from His most exalted station, saith unto me: "Would that my soul, O Prisoner, could be a ransom for Thy captivity, and my being, O wronged One, be sacrificed for the adversities Thou didst suffer!" (PM 40)

5. Bahá'u'lláh

I am he, O my God, who hath embraced Thy love and accepted all the adversities which the world can inflict, who hath offered up himself as a ransom for the sake of Thy loved ones, that they may ascend into the heavens of Thy knowledge and be drawn nearer unto Thee, and may soar in the atmosphere of Thy love and Thy good-pleasure. (PM 25)

I have accepted to be tried by manifold adversities for no purpose except to regenerate all that are in Thy heaven and on Thy earth. Whoso hath loved Thee, can never feel attached to his own self, except for the purpose of furthering Thy Cause... Acquaint them, moreover, with what He Who is the Origin of Thy most excellent titles hath, in His love for Thee, been willing to bear for the sake of the regeneration of their souls... (PM 198)

I yield Thee thanks, O my God, for that Thou hast offered me up as a sacrifice in Thy path, and made me a target for the arrows of afflictions as a token of Thy love for Thy servants, and singled me out for all manner of tribulation for the regeneration of Thy people. (PM 154)

D. The believers and the law of sacrifice

1. 'Abdu'l-Bahá, the perfect exemplar

Every man trained through the teachings of God and illumined
by the light of His guidance, who becomes a believer in God
and His signs and is enkindled with the fire of the love of
God, sacrifices the imperfections of nature for the sake of
divine perfections. Consequently, every perfect person, every
illumined, heavenly individual stands in the station of sacrifice.
(PUP 452)

Make me as dust in the pathway of Thy loved ones, and grant
that I may offer up my soul for the earth ennobled by the
footsteps of Thy chosen ones in Thy path, O Lord of Glory in
the Highest. (BP 333)

Be not sorrowful because of my imprisonment and lament
not over my difficulties; nay, rather, ask God to increase my
hardship in His path, for therein lies a wisdom which none are
able to comprehend save the near angels. (DAL74 95)

2. The believers

Reflect upon his holiness Job: What trials, calamities and
perplexities did he not endure! But these tests were like unto
the fire and his holiness Job was like unto pure gold. Assuredly,
gold is purified by being submitted to the fire and if it contain
any alloy or imperfection, it will disappear. That is the reason
why violent tests become the cause of the everlasting glory of
the righteous... (FG 39)

... may you seek to sacrifice yourselves in the pathway of
devotion to mankind. Even as Jesus Christ forfeited His
life, may you, likewise, offer yourselves in the threshold of
sacrifice for the betterment of the world; and just as Bahá'u'lláh
suffered severe ordeals and calamities nearly fifty years for
you, may you be willing to undergo difficulties and withstand
catastrophes for humanity in general. (DAL86 93)

Now is ther time, O ye beloved of the Lord, for ardent
endeavor. Struggle ye, and strive. And since the Ancient Beauty

was exposed by day and night on the field of martyrdom, let us in our turn labour hard, and hear and ponder the counsels of God; let us fling away our lives, and renounce our brief and numbered days. Let us turn our eyes away from empty fantasies of this world's divergent forms, and serve instead this pre-eminent purpose, this grand design. (SWA 275–276)

First, you must become united and agreed among yourselves. You must be exceedingly kind and loving toward each other, willing to forfeit life in the pathway of another's happiness. You must be ready to sacrifice your possessions in another's behalf. The rich among you must show compassion toward the poor, and the well-to-do must look after those in distress.... Your utmost desire must be to confer happiness upon each other. Each one must be the servant of the others, thoughtful of their comfort and welfare. In the path of God one must forget himself entirely. He must not consider his own pleasure but seek the pleasure of others. He must not desire glory not gifts of bounty for himself but seek these gifts and blessings for his brothers and sisters. It is my hope that that you may become like this, that you may attain to the supreme bestowal and be imbued with such spiritual qualities as to forget yourselves entirely and with heart and soul offer yourselves as sacrifices for the Blessed Perfection. (PUP 215)

E. The consequences of sacrifice

1. Transforms personal effort into spiritual qualities

As to the inconveniences you have experienced during the last ten years, the best consolation I can imagine for you is your own quotation of the Hidden Words, "My calamity is my providence." We must bear with one another. It is only through suffering that the nobility of character can make itself manifest. The energy we expend in enduring the intolerance of some individuals… is not lost. It is transformed into fortitude, steadfastness and magnanimity. The lives of Bahá'u'lláh and 'Abdu'l-Bahá are the best examples for this. Sacrifices in the path of one's religion produce always immortal results, "Out of the ashes rises the phoenix". (LG 604)

O peoples of the world! Whatsoever ye have offered up in the way of the One True God, ye shall indeed find preserved by God, the Preserver, intact at God's Holy Gate. (SWB 48)

2. Has a positive spiritual influence on others

It is difficult for us to understand these calamities when they come to us. Those who are firm in the Faith, know that the Hand of God protects them, and if something of this nature comes upon them, it is for some reason, which may have to do with the spiritual development of the one affected, of the spiritual development and welfare of the loved ones; or even for the melting of the hearts of non-Bahá'ís, who will be affected by the Divine Spirit, through the manner in which the Bahá'í meets such an ordeal. (LG 281)

To have sacrificed my life for the Manifestations of Thy Self, to have offered up my soul in the path of the Revealers of Thy wondrous Beauty, is to have sacrificed my spirit for Thy Spirit, my being for Thy Being, my glory for Thy Glory. It is as if I had offered up all these things for Thy sake, and for the sake of Thy loved ones. (PM 95-96)

3. Helps give meaning to tests and difficulties

The Master has often said that sorrows are like furrows, the deeper they go the more productive the land becomes. If this problem… should be settled other problems will arise. Are the friends to become discouraged or are they to follow the footsteps of the Master and consider them more as chances to show their tenacity of belief and spirit of sacrifice? (UD 422)

Peace of mind is gained by the centering of the spiritual consciousness on the Prophet of God; therefore you should study the spiritual Teachings, and receive the Water of Life from the Holy Utterances. Then by translating these high ideals into action, your entire character will be changed, and your mind will not only find peace, but your entire being will find joy and enthusiasm. (LG 112)

4. Releases spiritual power into the world

Should they attempt to conceal His light on the continent, He will assuredly rear His head in the midmost heart of the ocean and, raising His voice, proclaim: "I am the lifegiver of the world!" (DB 18)

No reference to such marvelous progress could fail to acknowledge the spiritual and social impact effected by the decade-long episode of persecution inflicted with such cruel excesses on our Iranian fellows-believers. Only in the future will the full consequence of their sacrifice be known, but we can clearly recognize its influence on the extraordinary success in proclaiming the Faith and in establishing good relations with governmental authorities and major non-governmental organizations around the world. (RM)

Undoubtedly, the highly esteemed American believers who bear the designation "spiritual descendants of the Dawn-breakers", know quite well that they must now seize their chance at this critical time to prove their capacity to endure that living sacrifice which, as Shoghi Effendi said, in contrast to dying, is required of them in the scriptures of our Faith.

May they be granted the celestial strength to pass, over and over again, the mental tests which 'Abdu'l-Bahá promised He would send them to purify them, thus enabling them to achieve their divinely conferred potential as a force for change in the world. (FG 151)

Man must forget his own selfish conditions that he may thus arise to the station of sacrifice. It should be to such a degree that if he sleep, it should not be for pleasure, but to rest the body in order to do better, to speak better, to explain more beautifully, to serve the servants of God and to prove the truths. When he remains awake, he should be attentive, serve the Cause of God and sacrifice his own stations for those of God. When he attains to this station, the confirmations of the Holy Spirit will surely reach him, and man with this power can withstand all who inhabit the earth. (JC 122-123)

One righteous act is endowed with a potency that can so elevate the dust as to cause it to pass beyond the heaven of heavens. It can tear every bond asunder, and hath the power to restore the force that hath spent itself and vanished. (GL 287)

Key to References

HW   The Hidden Words (1994)

GL   Gleanings from the Writings of Bahá'u'lláh (1983)

PT   Paris Talks (1995)

LG   Lights of Guidance (1999)

SS   Spiritual Survival (1998)

PM   Prayers and Meditations (1987)

SWA   Selections from the Writings of 'Abdu'l-Bahá (1997)

DAL74   The Divine Art of Living (1974)

DAL 86   The Divine Art of Living (1986)

FG   Fire and Gold, Benefiting from Life's Tests (1995)

JC   A Journey of Courage (2002)

BP   Bahá'í Prayers (2002)

SV   The Seven Valleys and the Four Valleys (1991)

SWB   Selections from the Writings of the Báb (1976)

BW   The Bahá'í World (vol. V, 1932–34)

DB   The Dispensation of Bahá'u'lláh (1981)

SW   Star of the West

UD   Unfolding Destiny (1981)

SAQ   Some Answered Questions (1994)

PDC   The Promised Day is Come (1980)

KI   Kitáb-i-Íqán The Book of Certitude (1989)

RM   Ridván Message, Universal House of Justice (1989)

KA   The Kítáb-i-Aqdas (1993)

PUP   The Promulgation of Universal Peace (1982)

www.ingramcontent.com/pod-product-compliance
Lightning Source LLC
Chambersburg PA
CBHW030307030426
42337CB00012B/615

9789888974516 5